States

VERMONT

by Bridget Parker

CAPSTONE PRESS
a capstone imprint

Next Page Books are published by Capstone Press,
1710 Roe Crest Drive, North Mankato, Minnesota 56003
www.mycapstone.com

Library of Congress Cataloging-in-Publication Data
Cataloging-in-publication information is on file with the Library of
Congress.
ISBN 978-1-5157-0433-1 (library binding)
ISBN 978-1-5157-0492-8 (paperback)
ISBN 978-1-5157-0544-4 (ebook PDF)

Editorial Credits
Jaclyn Jaycox, editor; Kazuko Collins and Katy LaVigne, designers;
Morgan Walters, media researcher; Tori Abraham, production specialist

Photo Credits
Capstone Press: Angi Gahler, map 4, 7; Corbis: Bettmann, middle
18; CriaImages.com: Jay Robert Nash Collection, top 18, top
19; Dreamstime: Carrienelson1, bottom 18; iStockphoto: Donald
Landwehrle, 7; Library of Congress: Prints and Photographs Division
Washington, 25; Newscom: CJ GUNTHER/EPA, 29, OrNewscom/Everett
Collection, bottom 19, Oronoz/Album, middle 19; One Mile Up, Inc.,
flag, seal 23; Shutterstock: Alexander Maksimov, bottom right 21, B.
Speckart, bottom right 20, Brittany Courville, 14, Christian Delbert, 28,
Daniel Prudek, bottom left 21, DonLand, cover, bottom left 8, bottom
right 8, 10, 15, 16, bottom 24, Erika J Mitchell, 5, Everett Historical,
27, Jason Patrick Ross, top left 21, Jay Boucher, middle right 21,
Jeffrey M. Frank, 26, jiawangkun, 9, 13, Joyce Vincent, 6, LEE
SNIDER PHOTO IMAGES, 11, Liz Van Steenburgh, top 24, Manamana,
middle left 21, margouillat photo, top right 21, Pinkcandy, 17, Stacy
Funderburke, top right 20, Stubblefield Photography, bottom left 20,
ZamadaS, top left 20; SuperStock: SuperStock, 12

All design elements by Shutterstock

Printed and bound in China.
0316/CA21600187
012016 009436F16

TABLE OF CONTENTS

Want to take your research further? Ask your librarian if your school subscribes to PebbleGo Next. If so, when you see this helpful symbol ⊕ throughout the book, log onto www.pebblegonext.com for bonus downloads and information.

LOCATION

Vermont is located in the northeastern United States. It is the second largest of the New England states. New York borders Vermont on the west, and Massachusetts lies to the south. The Connecticut River separates Vermont from New Hampshire to the east. The Canadian province of Quebec is north of Vermont. The capital of Vermont is Montpelier. With less than 8,000 people, Montpelier is the smallest U.S. state capital. Vermont's largest cities are Burlington, South Burlington, and Rutland.

PebbleGo Next Bonus!
To print and label
your own map, go to
www.pebblegonext.com
and search keywords:

UT MAP

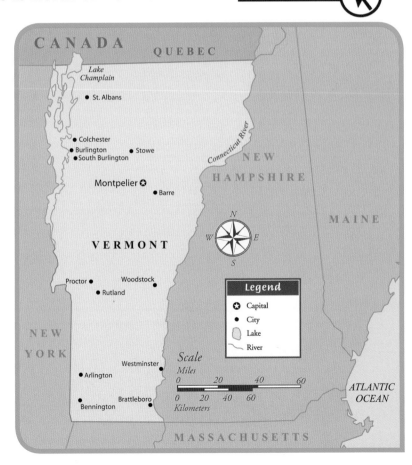

Montpelier was chosen as Vermont's state capital in 1805.

5

GEOGRAPHY

Vermont's land is marked by mountains and rolling hills. The Green Mountains stretch through the middle of Vermont from north to south. The state's highest point is in the Green Mountains. Mount Mansfield is 4,393 feet (1,339 meters) above sea level. The Piedmont lies at the foot of the Green Mountains and covers most of eastern Vermont. Lake Champlain, the sixth-largest freshwater lake in the United States, is in the northwest corner of the state.

PebbleGo Next Bonus!
To watch a video about
Rock of Ages, go to
www.pebblegonext.com
and search keywords:
VT VIDEO

A view from the top of Mount Mansfield

6

The Green Mountains are a part of the Appalachian Mountains.

Isle La Motte
Grand Isle
Missisquoi River
Lake Champlain
Lamoille River
▲ Mount Mansfield
Winooski River
Lake Memphremagog
NORTHEAST HIGHLANDS
Connecticut River
CHAMPLAIN VALLEY
Otter Creek
White River
GREEN MOUNTAINS
PIEDMONT
Lake Bomoseen
TACONIC MOUNTAINS
VALLEY OF VERMONT
Batten Kill

N
W E
S

Legend
▲ Highest Point
Lake
Mountain Range
River

Scale
Miles
0   20   40   60

0   20   40   60
Kilometers

WEATHER

Vermont has a cool climate throughout the year. The average summer temperature is 65 degrees Fahrenheit (18 degrees Celsius). Vermont winters are cold and snowy. In winter the average high temperature is 18°F (-8°C).

Average High and Low Temperatures (Burlington, VT)

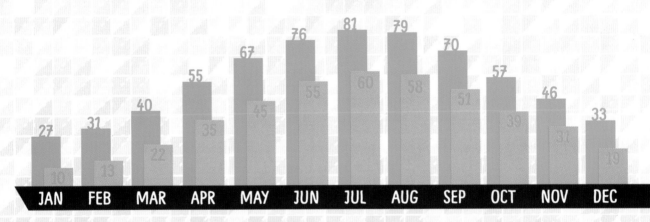

	JAN	FEB	MAR	APR	MAY	JUN	JUL	AUG	SEP	OCT	NOV	DEC
High	27	31	40	55	67	76	81	79	70	57	46	33
Low	10	13	22	35	45	55	60	58	51	39	31	19

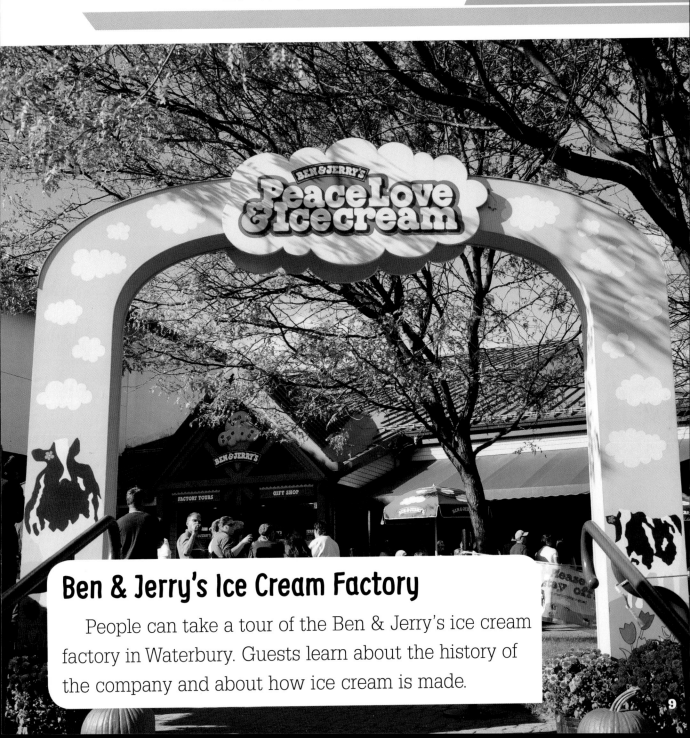

Ben & Jerry's Ice Cream Factory

People can take a tour of the Ben & Jerry's ice cream factory in Waterbury. Guests learn about the history of the company and about how ice cream is made.

Covered Bridges

Vermont has 107 covered bridges. Bridges were covered to protect them from the weather. All covered bridges in Vermont are protected by the state's board of historic sites.

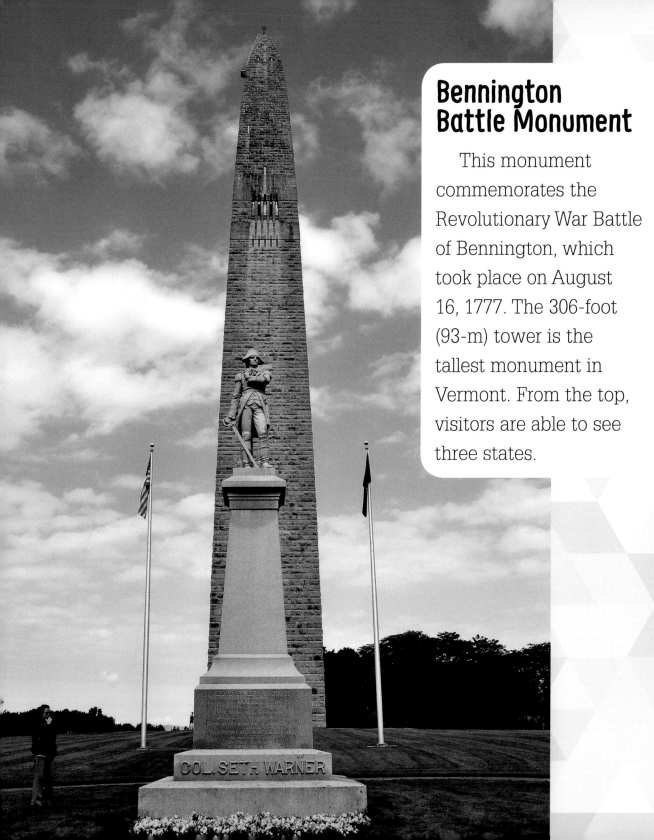

Bennington Battle Monument

This monument commemorates the Revolutionary War Battle of Bennington, which took place on August 16, 1777. The 306-foot (93-m) tower is the tallest monument in Vermont. From the top, visitors are able to see three states.

COL. SETH WARNER

HISTORY AND GOVERNMENT

John Stark leads New Hampshire soldiers at the Battle of Bennington during the Revolutionary War in 1777.

In the 1700s settlers were granted Vermont land called the New Hampshire Grants. After the French and Indian War (1754–1763), Great Britain gained control of the area. During the Revolutionary War (1775–1783), settlers from the New Hampshire Grants declared themselves an independent republic. They named their republic the Free and Independent State of Vermont. After defeating Great Britain, the 13 colonies became the United States of America. Vermont was allowed to join the United States and became the 14th state.

Vermont's government has three branches. The legislative branch makes the state's laws. It includes the 30-member Senate and the 150-member House of Representatives. The governor is the head of the executive branch, which makes sure the state's laws are carried out. Judges and their courts make up the judicial branch.

The House and Senate Chambers of Vermont's capitol are the oldest in the United States to still be in their original condition.

INDUSTRY

Tourism is a top industry in Vermont. Skiing is the state's top tourist activity. Mountains near Stowe and Killington are among Vermont's most popular skiing and snowboarding areas. Vermont is home to one of the world's largest snowboard companies, Burton Snowboards in Burlington. During fall many tourists come to Vermont to see the colorful leaves.

Vermont's largest factories produce electrical equipment and electronic parts. Other factories produce machinery, metal parts, and machine tools.

Vermont produces an average of 1.2 million gallons of maple syrup each year.

Vermont's industry also comes from its natural resources. Vermont is the country's largest producer of maple syrup. Farmers also grow apples, hay, vegetables, greenhouse plants, and Christmas trees. Vermont's trees are used in construction and to make furniture, paper, and pulp products. Vermont mines produce granite, marble, and slate.

Hotels, motels, resorts, and other tourist-related services provide jobs to thousands of Vermonters.

POPULATION

Most Vermonters are white. Many of these Vermonters have English or French backgrounds. In the mid-1800s, many Italians also moved to Vermont to work in the stone quarries. Barre still has a large Italian population. Burlington has the state's largest Hispanic and Asian populations, which together make up about 3 percent of the state's population. Fewer than 6,000 Vermonters are African-American, which make up the third-largest ethnic group. Vermont had a large American Indian population before European settlers came. Today only about 2,000 American Indians live in Vermont. Most of them belong to the Abenaki tribe.

Population by Ethnicity

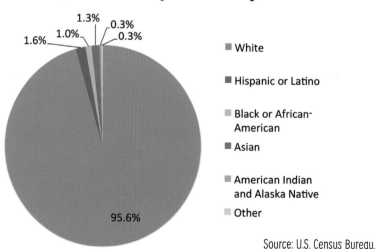

- 1.6%
- 1.0%
- 1.3%
- 0.3%
- 0.3%
- 95.6%

■ White

■ Hispanic or Latino

■ Black or African-American

■ Asian

■ American Indian and Alaska Native

■ Other

Source: U.S. Census Bureau.

FAMOUS PEOPLE

Robert Frost (1874–1963) was a beloved poet who wrote about New England life. He helped start the Bread Loaf Writers' Conference at Middlebury College. He was born in California and lived in Vermont for many years.

John Deere (1804–1886) invented the first steel plow. His company continues to manufacture plows and tractors. He was born in Rutland and raised in Middlebury.

Ben Cohen (1951–) and **Jerry Greenfield** (1950–) opened their first Ben & Jerry's ice cream shop in Burlington in 1978. It didn't take long for their ice cream to become world famous.

Calvin Coolidge (1872–1933) was the 30th U.S. president (1923–1929). His nickname was "Silent Cal." He was born in Plymouth Notch.

Ethan Allen (1738–1789) was a Revolutionary War hero who formed the Green Mountain Boys. He led them in taking Fort Ticonderoga from the British (1775). He was born in Connecticut.

Katherine Paterson (1932–) is the two-time winner of the Newbery Medal and the National Book Award. She has written many novels, including the classic *Bridge to Terabithia*. She lives in Barre.

STATE SYMBOLS

Tree

sugar maple

Flower

red clover

Bird

hermit thrush

Animal

Morgan horse

PebbleGo Next Bonus! To make a dessert using maple syrup, highly produced in Vermont, go to www.pebblegonext.com and search keywords:

VT RECIPE

Butterfly

monarch

Pie

apple pie

Mineral

talc

Fruit

apple

Insect

honeybee

Gem

grossular garnet

FAST FACTS

STATEHOOD
1791

CAPITAL ☆
Montpelier

LARGEST CITY •
Burlington

SIZE
9,217 square miles (23,872 square kilometers)
land area (2010 U.S. Census Bureau)

POPULATION
626,630 (2013 U.S. Census estimate)

STATE NICKNAME
Green Mountain State

STATE MOTTO
"Freedom and Unity"

STATE SEAL

Vermont adopted its state seal in 1937. The seal includes a pine tree, a spear, a cow, and four sheaves of wheat. Wooded hills represent the Green Mountains. Wavy lines at the top and bottom of the seal stand for water and sky. The words "Vermont" and the state motto, "Freedom and Unity," are at the bottom of the seal.

PebbleGo Next Bonus! To print and color your own flag, go to www.pebblegonext.com and search keywords: UT FLAG

STATE FLAG

The current Vermont flag was adopted in 1919. The flag has a blue background with the state coat of arms in the middle. The pine tree on the coat of arms represents Vermont's forests. To the left of the tree are three sheaves of wheat to represent agriculture. The cow stands for the animals used in agriculture. Pine boughs wrap around the shield. A deer's head at the top of the shield stands for Vermont's wildlife. A red banner at the bottom of the shield reads "Vermont, Freedom and Unity."

MINING PRODUCTS

crushed stone, sand and gravel, dimension stone, gemstones

MANUFACTURED GOODS

computer and electronic parts, food products, machinery

FARM PRODUCTS

dairy products, greenhouse plants, hay, vegetables, maple syrup

PebbleGo Next Bonus!
To learn the lyrics to
the state song, go to
www.pebblegonext.com
and search keywords:
UT SONG

VERMONT TIMELINE

1000   Abenaki and Mahican people are living in Vermont.

1609   French explorer Samuel de Champlain sails into Lake Champlain.

1620   The Pilgrims establish a colony in the New World in present-day Massachusetts.

1724   Fort Dummer becomes the first permanent European settlement in Vermont.

1749   Vermont becomes known as the New Hampshire Grants.

1775 Ethan Allen and the Green Mountain Boys capture Fort Ticonderoga during the Revolutionary War.

1777 Settlers from the New Hampshire Grants declare their independence.

1791 Vermont becomes the 14th state on March 4.

1823 The Champlain-Hudson Canal links Vermont to New York City.

1861–1865 The Union and the Confederacy fight the Civil War. Soldiers from Vermont fight for the Union.

1881 Vermonter Chester Arthur becomes president of the United States on September 20.

1914–1918 World War I is fought; the United States enters the war in 1917.

1923 On August 2 Vermont native Calvin Coolidge becomes president of the United States.

1927 A huge flood on November 2–4 kills 84 people in Vermont.

1957 IBM opens a plant in Essex Junction.

1968 Vermont bans billboards.

1970 On April 4 the Vermont legislature passes a law to protect the state's scenic landscape. It is the first law of its kind to be passed anywhere in the United States.

1984 Madeleine M. Kunin is elected Vermont's first female governor.

2011 In August Tropical Storm Irene causes major floods, washes away bridges, and causes three deaths in Vermont.

2014 Vermont closes its Yankee Nuclear Power Plant. Before that, the state depended on nuclear power for most of its electricity.

2015 U.S. Senator Bernie Sanders from Vermont joins the presidential race.

Glossary

commemorate *(kuh-MEM-uh-rate)*—doing something special to honor and remember a person or event

ethnic *(ETH-nik)*—related to a group of people and their culture

executive *(ig-ZE-kyuh-tiv)*—the branch of government that makes sure laws are followed

industry *(IN-duh-stree)*—a business which produces a product or provides a service

judicial *(joo-DISH-uhl)*—to do with the branch of government that explains and interprets the laws

legislature *(LEJ-iss-lay-chur)*—a group of elected officials who have the power to make or change laws for a country or state

province *(PROV-uhnss)*—a district or a region of some countries

pulp *(PUHLP)*—a mixture of ground up paper and water

quarry *(KWOR-ee)*—a place where stone or other minerals are dug from the ground

sea level *(SEE LEV-uhl)*—the average level of the surface of the ocean, used as a starting point from which to measure the height or depth of any place

sheaf *(SHEEF)*—a bundle

tourism *(TOOR-i-zuhm)*—the business of taking care of visitors to a country or place

Read More

Bailer, Darice. *What's Great About Vermont?* Our Great States. Minneapolis: Lerner Publications, 2016.

Dornfeld, Margaret. *Vermont.* It's My State! New York: Marshall Cavendish Benchmark, 2013.

Ganeri, Anita. *United States of America: A Benjamin Blog and His Inquisitive Dog Guide.* Country Guides. Chicago: Heinemann Raintree, 2015.

Internet Sites

FactHound offers a safe, fun way to find Internet sites related to this book. All of the sites on FactHound have been researched by our staff.

Here's all you do:

Visit *www.facthound.com*

Type in this code: 9781515704331

 Check out projects, games and lots more at **www.capstonekids.com**

Critical Thinking Using the Common Core

1. What is the highest point in Vermont? How high above sea level is it? (Key Ideas and Details)

2. In the mid-1800s many Italians moved to Vermont to work in the stone quarries. What is a quarry? (Craft and Structure)

3. Tourism is a top industry in Vermont. If you were to visit, what types of things would you want to do? (Integration of Knowledge and Ideas)

Index